AI IN THE WORLD

AI IN THE ENVIRONMENT

WRITTEN BY
BERNADETTE PARKHURST-SMITH

KidHaven
PUBLISHING

Published in 2026 by
KidHaven Publishing, an Imprint of Greenhaven Publishing, LLC
2544 Clinton St., Buffalo, NY 14224

Written by: Bernadette Parkhurst-Smith
Edited by: Sadie Hallworth
Designed by: Ker Ker Lee

Cataloging-in-Publication Data
Names: Parkhurst-Smith, Bernadette.
Title: AI in the environment / Bernadette Parkhurst-Smith.
Description: Buffalo, NY : KidHaven Publishing, 2026. | Series: AI in the world | Includes glossary and index.
Identifiers: ISBN 9781534551732 (pbk.) | ISBN 9781534551749 (library bound) | ISBN 9781534551756 (ebook)
Subjects: LCSH: Environmental sciences--Juvenile literature. | Artificial intelligence--Juvenile literature. | Artificial intelligence--Environmental applications--Juvenile literature.
Classification: LCC GE115.P375 2026 | DDC 550--dc23

Printed in China

CPSIA compliance information: Batch #QW26KH: For further information contact Greenhaven Publishing LLC at 1-844-317-7404.

Please visit our website, www.greenhavenpublishing.com.
For a free color catalog of all our high-quality books,
call toll free 1-844-317-7404
or fax 1-844-317-7405.

Photo Credits – Images courtesy of Shutterstock.com, unless otherwise stated.

Cover & Recurring – HuHu, Vadim Almiev, Huticon, Olga S L, klee048, PixieMe, VVQ. 2–3 – NovitaSari Image. 4–5 – Gorodenkoff, Bilanol, Toa55. 6–7 – Inside Creative House. 8–9 – Maples Images, AlexLMX. 10–11 – AlvaroGO, Joe McDonald, Wayne Tyler Leiseberg. 12–13 – metamorworks, patpitchaya. 14–15 – metamorworks, Suwin66. 16–17 – Vladimka production, Gorodenkoff. 18–19 – TAUFIK ART, K I Photography. 20–21 – PARALAXIS, Reforestation Collection, Eduardo Cota. 22–23 – IM Imagery, Make more Aerials, 1st footage.

CONTENTS

WORDS THAT LOOK LIKE <u>THIS</u> CAN BE FOUND IN THE GLOSSARY ON PAGE 24.

WHAT IS AI?

When we learn things and find ways to solve problems, we are showing intelligence. Scientists have made machines that learn and solve problems. This shows artificial intelligence, or AI.

Earth is warming up, which is causing climate change. This is creating many problems for the humans, plants, and animals on our planet. Scientists are finding ways for AI to help us.

As our climate changes, it can cause some extreme weather.

DATASET DICTIONARY

Here are some key words you may need to help you understand AI.

Algorithms

sets of steps machines follow to solve a problem or complete a task

Data

information

Predictions

guesses about things that could happen based on evidence and facts

Computer Programs

lists of instructions that a computer can understand

Machines

pieces of equipment used to complete tasks

Sensors

devices that can sense things such as light, temperature, movement, or sound

Hint: Remember that AI is short for artificial intelligence!

SORTING RECYCLING

When we recycle things, they can be used to make new things instead of being sent to a landfill. Landfills are becoming too full of trash. Recycling is one way we can help our planet.

RECYCLING MUST BE SORTED INTO DIFFERENT GROUPS.

Some cities have found a way to use AI to help them sort recycling. AI can recognize different materials to be recycled. AI can even use robots to help separate the different items.

USING AI AND ROBOTS CAN MAKE SORTING RECYCLING QUICKER AND SAFER.

HELPING HABITATS

Camera traps are very useful for tracking wildlife and studying habitats. Scientists set up camera traps in the wild. The camera traps take photos and videos of animals that set off the sensors.

A habitat is where a living thing makes its home.

AI is sometimes better than people at analyzing images by spotting patterns and differences. Conservationists can use AI to spot changes in habitats and track endangered species.

Scientists can use AI to compare many different photos and videos.

MAKING PREDICTIONS

AI technology needs data to work. Scientists put in the data. Then, AI computer programs spot patterns in the data and make predctions.

When you see a pattern, you might be able to predict what comes next. AI can make these predictions faster than humans can. We can use AI to make predictions about important things such as the weather.

AI that makes predictions is called predictive AI.

WEATHER WATCHERS

As our climate changes, the weather is becoming more extreme. It is very important to know when there will be hurricanes, wildfires, or tornadoes. Early warnings mean people can evacuate before it is too dangerous.

When we make predictions about the weather, it is called a forecast.

AI uses data from the past to make predictions about the weather in the future. When meteorologists work with AI, they can predict a hurricane or tornado's path sooner.

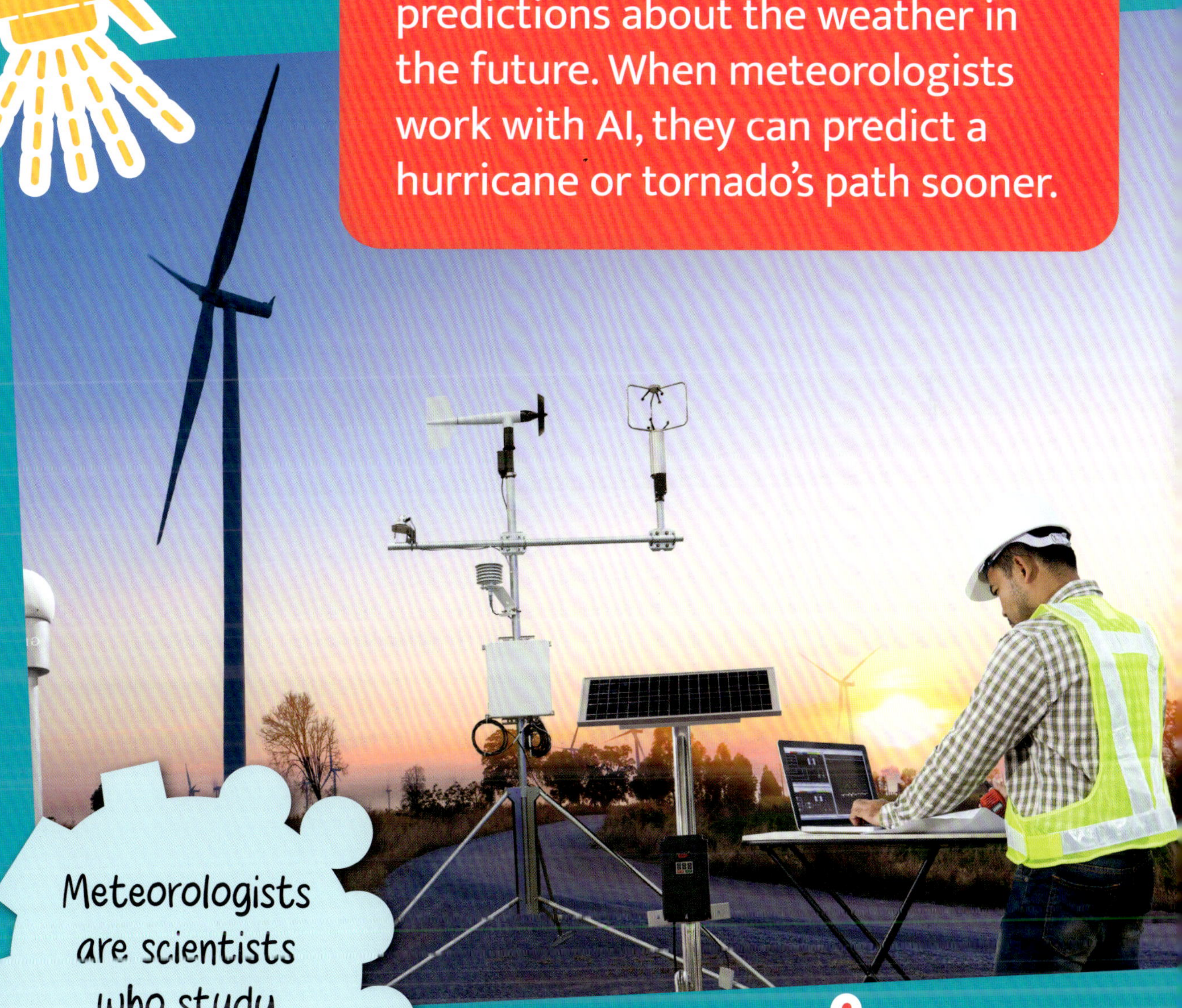

Meteorologists are scientists who study the weather.

WIND POWER

Renewable energy is energy from things that nature will replace. Wind is a source of renewable energy. When the wind spins a wind turbine, it creates electricity.

Renewable energy is better for the environment than non-renewable energy.

Wind turbines can only make electricity when enough wind is blowing the right way. Some turbines use sensors and algorithms that predict the weather. Engineers can then make the turbines more efficient.

CLEANING THE OCEANS

Some groups clean up plastic from the world's oceans and rivers. Boats pull long nets through patches of trash.

AI-powered cameras scan the ocean surface for plastic. The cameras can spot plastic in the ocean a lot quicker than humans can, so even more plastic can be cleaned up.

The plastic that is collected from the oceans can then be recycled.

REGROW THE RAINFOREST

Rainforests are very important to our planet. AI can help scientists track deforestation using satellite photos. AI algorithms can predict which areas are most at risk of illegal deforestation before it happens.

Drones are flying robots. Some scientists are using drones to drop seeds to regrow forests in Brazil. AI tells the drones where to go and how many seeds they need to drop.

drone

INTO THE FUTURE

AI is powered by big data centers. These centers use a lot of water and energy. Some people want data centers to use less energy and be more efficient.

data center

Some people want AI companies to recycle water from their data centers. They also want these companies to use renewable energy to power their data centers. This would make AI more environmentally friendly.

GLOSSARY

conservationists people who protect things found in nature, including wildlife

deforestation the cutting down and removal of trees in a forest

efficient able to get the most out of something in the best way possible, often by using less energy

endangered species living things that are in danger of going extinct

evacuate move people away from a dangerous place

illegal against the law

landfill an area of land where trash is sent

source where something comes from

temperature how hot or cold something is

tracking closely following something

INDEX